Literacy and Language

Anthology  2
Book 1

Janey Pursglove and **Charlotte Raby**

Series developed by **Ruth Miskin**

Contents

OXFORD

UNIVERSITY PRESS

Sister

FOR SALE

Adrian Bradbury

Have you got a big sister? *I* have. I used to wish
I hadn't. I once got so fed up I made up an advert.

For Sale

Big Sister   11 human years old

- Answers to the name 'Molly'
- £5 or nearest offer.

I tried to put it in the local paper. I phoned them up.

"You have to be 18 to put in an advert," they said.

"I am," I answered in my deepest voice.

"Hmm, 18 months maybe," they replied. Then they put the phone down. What a cheek!

It wasn't that Molly was nasty to me or anything. As sisters go, she was all right, I suppose. But then she got the

Mummying Bug.

It all started on my sixth birthday. Mum baked me a yummy chocolate cake, with thick toffee icing and six blue candles on top. I made my usual wish (to be the first schoolboy to land on Mars) then took an **almighty** breath and blew them all out.

All except one. I had another go. Still no luck. "Try again, Tom," Molly said, and this time she leaned over and blew too. The candle went out.

"Well done, Tom!" cried Mum happily. "Now cut the cake."

'Cool,' I thought. 'I can cut myself a

whopping great slice

and eat till I burst.'

I tried. I *really* tried. But the icing on top was so thick I couldn't get the knife through it.

Before I could stop her, Molly had taken it out of my hands. "Here, Tom, let me help."

"Whatever would you do without your big sister, eh, Tom?" said Mum.

'Eat more cake!' I thought.

From that moment on, Molly was like my spare mum. Every day as we left for school, she was there at the door. She tied up my laces, wiped jam off my face and dragged a comb through my hair.

"However would you manage without me, eh, Tom?"

Then... **Year 2. Day 1.**

Big Trouble!

Mum, Molly and I were walking to school. A group of kids from my new class were with us. When we got to the crossing, Mrs Brown, the lollipop lady, stopped the traffic and waved us over. Molly, as usual, reached out and grabbed my hand.

I yanked it free. "Get off me, will you? I'm not a baby!"

Mum went bananas. "How dare you talk to your sister like that?" she yelled. "She's only being helpful."

So from then on, I kept my big mouth shut. I spoke inside my head, in thought bubbles, like in comics.

Every day, Molly insisted on walking me to my classroom and straightening my tie before I went in.

"Thanks," I muttered. But in my head was a bubble with big red letters saying:

Even worse, at lunchtimes she always came over and cut up my meat. I could feel my cheeks burning as everyone looked. Embarrassing or what?

"Is that better?" she'd ask.

It went on like that. Every time I spotted her coming I checked my tie, my shoelaces, my mouth, my hair. Anything to keep her off me. That was when I decided to sell her.

One lunchtime in the playground, I was playing soldiers with Jack and Amin, as usual. We were on a secret mission behind enemy lines. I wriggled under the barbed wire and tripped up Big Bad Rory Smith from 5L as he dribbled past with the football. Down he went.

CRASH!

The ground shook.

"Who did that? Who tripped me up?" He was back on his feet, and he was **fuming**. Then he spotted me on the ground. "Oh, it was you, was it? Little Baby Tom! Can't even wash his own face!"

Then everyone else joined in. "Baby Tom! Baby Tom!"

I lay there, blinking back the tears. Rory stood
over me, laughing his smelly socks off. They were all
laughing.

Then suddenly everything went quiet. A shadow
loomed over Rory.

"Lay – off – my – brother."

She didn't even raise her voice. She didn't need to.

One look at her was enough. She looked like a volcano about to erupt. Eyes popping out, fists clenched. SCARY!

All that was missing was steam shooting out of her ears. The crowd backed off. Rory **scarpered**.

"Thanks sis," I mumbled.

Whatever would I do without you?

After that, Molly let me take care of myself. She'd heard what the other kids called me, and she worked out why. She stopped being a spare mum and went back to being just a really annoying, bossy big sister.

So now I do my own laces, cut my own meat and stand up for myself. I even learned to tie my own tie. I must admit I don't *always* get it right.

Parents and their Young

How do young children learn to survive in our world?

First, human parents need to show their children how to walk, talk and keep warm. They also teach them how to stay safe, what to eat and how to cross the road.

Is it the same in the animal kingdom?

Well, yes, and no!

Like humans, almost all animals look after their young until they think they can **survive** on their own. The father's job is often to go out to find food and bring it home. Meanwhile, the mother will stay with her young.

Keeping the young safe

A young kangaroo is called a **joey**. When the joey is born, it is tiny – too small to move safely on the ground. To keep it from harm, its mother has a special pouch. The joey lives and grows in the pouch until it is big enough to stand on its own two feet.

Some young fish hide from danger in their mother's mouth. This is because young fish have no defences. The mother lets them out to play when the danger has passed.

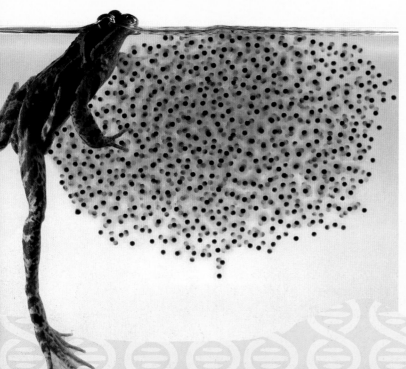

Like humans, many creatures will risk their own lives to **protect** their young. A male bullfrog will stand up to a snake or a bird if they get too close to its tadpoles!

Learning to survive

Young hunters, such as lion and tiger cubs, learn many of their skills from their mother. She'll teach them how to sniff out **prey**, how to follow it without being seen, and finally how to kill.

However, some parents don't want to stay with their young. Some cuckoos **abandon** their eggs in another bird's nest, and let them do all the hard work!

Other parents aren't able to look after their young. A sea turtle lays her eggs on land, but has to leave them because of the cold. So she digs a hole, lays the eggs in the bottom and then covers them with sand again. The sand helps to keep the eggs warm until they hatch. It also stops them from being eaten by other animals.

Mother lays eggs in hole on the beach

Mother covers eggs and leaves

They return to the beach

Eggs hatch

Turtles head straight for the sea

When the young turtles hatch, they head straight for the sea. This is because they know by instinct exactly where to go. If they survive and grow into adults they will return to the same beach to lay their eggs.

Some **reptiles** lay thousands of eggs. This is because they know that many of their young will not survive. However, sea turtles who do survive and become adults may live to the age of 60, and many will produce thousands of eggs of their own.

Tiger

A colour splasher
A stripe flasher
An eye gleamer
A wide beamer
A sleek sprinter
A smart hunter
A lone prowler
A loud growler
A night walker
A deer stalker
A soft sneaker
A strong striker
A swift pouncer
A quick bouncer
A fierce snarler
A cruel mauler
A great fighter
A bad biter
A meat eater
A man hater

Usha Kishore

River

boat-carrier
bark-lapper
home-provider
tree-reflector
leaf-catcher
field-wanderer
stone-smoother
fast-mover
gentle-stroller
sun-sparkler
sea-seeker

June Crebbin

Don't Call Alligator Long-Mouth Till You Cross River

Call alligator long-mouth

call alligator saw-mouth

call alligator pushy-mouth

call alligator scissors-mouth

call alligator raggedy-mouth

call alligator bumpy-bum

call alligator all dem rude word

but better wait

    till you cross river.

John Agard

Journey to the Deep

The sea bed is full of life.
Let's take a trip down to have a look...

The Shallows

Shallow water, near the coast, is quite warm. The sun can easily reach the sea bed. Lots of colourful plants and creatures live here. We can dive down to see them.

Sponges, urchins and blue sea stars cling to coral reefs.

21

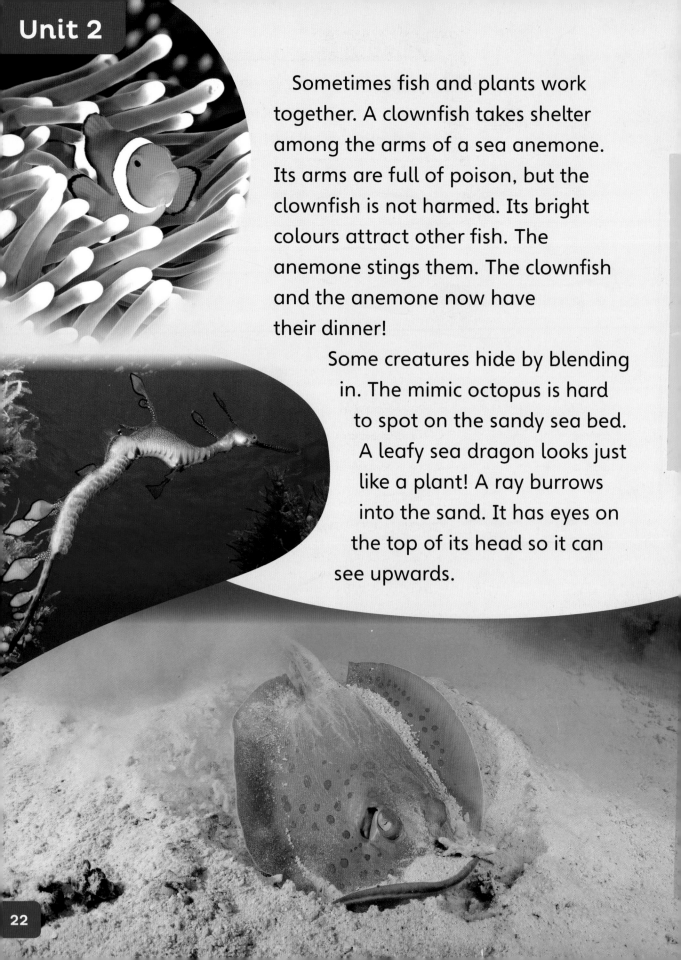

Sometimes fish and plants work together. A clownfish takes shelter among the arms of a sea anemone. Its arms are full of poison, but the clownfish is not harmed. Its bright colours attract other fish. The anemone stings them. The clownfish and the anemone now have their dinner!

Some creatures hide by blending in. The mimic octopus is hard to spot on the sandy sea bed. A leafy sea dragon looks just like a plant! A ray burrows into the sand. It has eyes on the top of its head so it can see upwards.

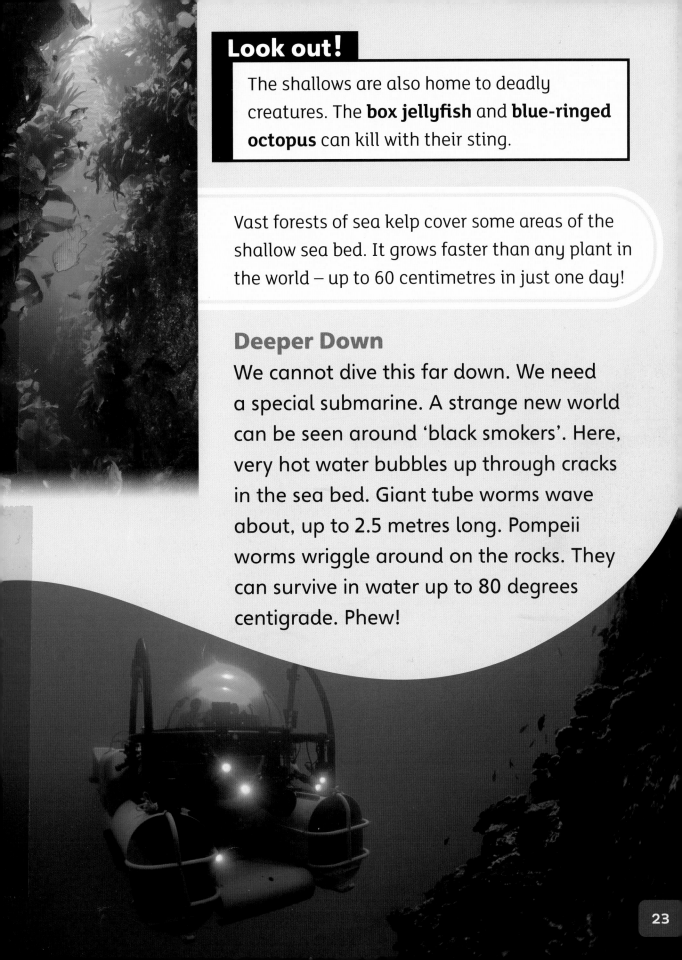

Look out!

The shallows are also home to deadly creatures. The **box jellyfish** and **blue-ringed octopus** can kill with their sting.

Vast forests of sea kelp cover some areas of the shallow sea bed. It grows faster than any plant in the world – up to 60 centimetres in just one day!

Deeper Down

We cannot dive this far down. We need a special submarine. A strange new world can be seen around 'black smokers'. Here, very hot water bubbles up through cracks in the sea bed. Giant tube worms wave about, up to 2.5 metres long. Pompeii worms wriggle around on the rocks. They can survive in water up to 80 degrees centigrade. Phew!

The Deep

The deepest ocean is far beyond the reach of the sun. Down here, all is inky black. No plants can live.

Creatures move in slow motion to save energy. Food mostly comes drifting down from above – the bodies of dead creatures that sink down to the bottom.

But some fish are still hunters. The hairy angler fish has its own light! The light dangles like the bait on a fishing rod and lures fish into its deadly jaws.

The deepest part of the sea bed is over seven miles down. Only three men have ever been there, including James Cameron – director of the film *Titanic*.